絵で おぼえる 英会話

REAL Talking by Ellie Oh
© Ellie Oh, 2011

Originally published by Woongjin Think Big Co., Ltd. in Korea.
All rights reserved.
Japanese copyright © 2020 by Bunkyosha Co., Ltd.,
Japanese translation rights arranged with Woongjin Think Big Co., Ltd. through Danny Hong Agency

アレ、英語で どう言うんだっけ… におさらば!

 「とっさの一言」が口からスラスラ出てくるように

「えーと、アレ、英語でどう言うんだっけ…」。そんなふうに、**いざという時に英語が出てこず、悔しい思いをしたことはありませんか?** やみくもに暗記するだけでは実践的な英会話力は身につきません。

I'm doin' so well.

After

しかしこの本ならあっという間に、**とっさの場面でも口から英語がスラスラ出てくる**ようになります。

その秘密は、**本番さながらのシチュエーションを体験しながら表現を覚えられるユニークな構成**=「Real Talking」にあります。

この本の原書は、世界的に絶大な支持を誇る英語学習の「会話」シリーズ第一作として 2011 年に韓国で発売され、6ヶ月以上にわたりランキング1位を独占するなど、大反響を呼んだ超ロング・ベストセラー。難しい問題や解説は一切ナシ! ストーリーを楽しむだけで、1人でも手軽に取り組めます。

 どんなレベルからでも、自分のペースで続けられる

フレンドリーで物怖じしない、そんな主人公 Anna になりきって、日常的な英会話に触れてみてください。**英語がみるみる自分のものになっていく感覚**に驚くはず! 留学したり語学学校に通ったりしなくても「Real Talking」メソッドで英語力アップ間違いなし。

一度は学校で英語を習ったあなたに、これ以上新しい文法や難しい英単語は必要ありません。

I'd like to get a refund, please.

必要なのは、すでに知っている英語を日常の中に取り込む練習だけ。本書はそんなあなたの力強い味方になるはずです。

1

5つ の特長

1 Fun!
楽しい

本なのに気分はさながら海外旅行！
Real Talking では実際の場面を体感
できるから、楽しくマンガを読むだ
けでフレーズがスラスラ覚えられます。
主人公 Anna と一緒に、さあ出かけましょう！

2

2 Useful!
役に立つ

今日から使える簡単フレーズが
盛り沢山! そのほか海外Q&A
や関連単語も併せて覚えられる
から、実生活で生きてくる本当
の英語力が身につきます!

3 Easy!
カンタン

飽き性の人も心配無用! 全てのセリフをアメリ
カ人ナレーターが読み上げた付属音声や、14
日間完成のおすすめ学習スケジュールがつい
ているから、手軽なのに1人でもしっかり成果
が出ます!

4 Only English!
本格的

本文は英語だけ! でも心配はいりません。初めて言
葉を学ぶ子どものように、ストーリーを楽しむうちに
自然と英語を英語のまま理解できるようになります。
シンプルな日常会話とはいえ、英語を英語で覚える
ことは真の英語力向上への最短ルートです。

5 Repeat!
忘れない

用途別に活用できる4種の付属音声のほか、スペ
リングチェックにも使えるミニテスト、ディクテーショ
ン編もついているから、何度もリピート学習できて
フレーズを忘れる心配はありません。

わたしも
感動の声、
続々！

{ **Real Talking** } で

話せるようになりました！

VOICE 01
▶20代 男性

3年前イギリスに旅行したとき、思うように英語でコミュニケーションが取れず悔しい思いをしました。ところが、この本に載っているフレーズは簡単でシンプルなものばかりだったので、**難しく考えていた英会話のハードルが下がり、やる気がわきました。**

簡単な英語で海外旅行を乗り切っている友人のことが羨ましかったのですが、Annaを見て、そのコツが分かった気がします。私も彼女のように堂々と英語を話せるよう、この本で頑張ります！

VOICE 02
▶20代 女性

VOICE 03
▶20代 女性

フレーズを覚えた後には確認テストでチェックできるので、**自分の苦手な部分がわかって便利です。**

まさに日常生活で必要なフレーズが詰まっています。いろんな場所を舞台に、よくあるシチュエーションがマンガ形式で学べるうえ、**関連単語やコラムもあるのでとても助かりました。**

VOICE 04
▶20代 男性

必須フレーズがこの一冊に凝縮されているので手軽に
読めてよかったです。丁寧かつユーモラスなイラスト
が付いているおかげで、**実際のシチュエーション
をイメトレできるのが最高です!**

▶ 10代 男性

▶ 30代 女性

マンガ形式で日常会話が学べて、**辞書や文法書
なしに気軽に読めて助かっています。** Anna
の海外での日常を覗いている気分になれるので、
「Real Talking」という呼び名も納得です!

**ストーリー仕立てになっているのが気に入り、
一気に最後まで読んでしまいました。** Annaと
一緒にフレーズを学ぶうちに、「はやく海外に行って
実践したい!」と思えるようになりました。

▶ 10代 女性

▶ 40代 女性

小学生の娘と楽しく読みました。 一緒に練習
して、実際に旅行先で実践してみたいと思います。

▶ 40代 男性

シチュエーションを思い浮かべながら Annaの真似を
して自分でも口に出して練習してみたところ、**旅先で
実際に店員さんと話をする時に口から自然と
英語が出てきました。** 今はもっといろんな場面で
実践してみたくて、口がうずうずしています!

CONTENTS

付属音声について

リアル Real

BGMや効果音入りで、まるでその場にいるかのような没入感を味わいながら学べる音声です。臨場感を演出するため、テキストに記載のない相槌なども一部収録しています。

シャドーイング Shadowing

解説や単語の説明（斜線部分が該当）が入った、リピート練習用の音声です。ゆっくり、はっきりとした読み上げで、発音の確認にも最適です。

ロールプレイ
Role Play

Annaの音声のみを取り除いた音声です。Annaになりきって登場人物たちと会話してみましょう。

レッツレビュー
Let's Review

各スキットの重要フレーズの確認クイズの音声です。学習後に活用し、理解度をチェックしましょう。

14日間で
誰でも
ペラペラに！

Real Talking

おすすめ
学習スケジュール

14日間完成

START!

Day 1	Day 2	Day 3
12~144 ページ	12~45 ページ	46~75 ページ

Day 4	Day 5	Day 6	Day 7
76~109 ページ	110~144 ページ	12~75 ページ	76~144 ページ

Day 8	Day 9	Day 10	Day 11
145~175 ページ	176~201 ページ	202~231 ページ	232~263 ページ

Day 12	Day 13	Day 14
12~75 ページ	76~144 ページ	12~144 ページ

FINISH!

本書の使い方

1 想像する -

場面ごとに「使ってみたいフレーズ」「知らなかったフレーズ」を頭に浮かべながら、ページをめくってみましょう。

2 聞く -

音声を聞きながら、最初は心の中で→慣れたら口に出して、セリフをまねてみましょう。1回20分程度なので、1日2回、通勤や通学などのすきま時間を活用するのがオススメ！

3 話してみる - - - - - - - - - - - - - - - - - - -

音声を聞きながら、ナレーターの抑揚や間の取り方などをまねて声に出します。慣れてきたら本を見ずに挑戦してみましょう。

4 書き取る -

Dictation Book（145ページ以降）を使って、ディクテーション（ページ下部参照）の練習をしてみましょう。まずは Let's Review ①〜④の空欄を使って練習をしてから Dictation Book に進むのがおすすめです。リスニングだけでなくスペリングも鍛えられます。

5 会話する -

友人や家族と役割を分担して話してみましょう。お互いのスピーキング力向上につながります。1人の場合は、音声を活用して実際の会話のつもりで話します。自分の声を録音して、発音をチェックするのも効果的。

英語力がさらにアップ！
ディクテーションとは？

「ディクテーション」とは、音声を聞いて行う書き取り練習のこと。リスニングにもスペリングの強化にも効果的です。まず音声を聞き、そのまま書き取ります。1回で全て書きとれなければ、30秒程度で区切り、繰り返し聞いて完成させます。最後までわからない部分は、その理由がリスニング（聞き取れなかった）なのか、スペリング（綴りがわからなかった）なのかを確認しましょう。同じ教材でくりかえし行うのがオススメです。

12

Don't be nervous.
They just ask your name
to call you when your
order is ready.

Useful phrases when ordering

ABOUT COFFEE

brewed coffee

ice blended

espresso

non-coffee drink

extra hot

decaf
= no caffeine

skinny
= non-fat = has skim milk

17

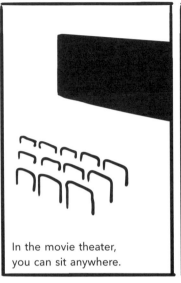

In the movie theater, you can sit anywhere.

Excuse me. Is this seat taken?

No, go ahead.

Wow, it's amazing!

I'd better get some brunch.

18

MOVIE CATEGORIES & GENRES

Science Fiction & Fantasy

Family & Kids

Action & Adventure

Romance

Mystery & Suspense

Animation

20

Are you ready to order?

BRUNCH MENU

Three Eggs & Pancakes $12.50

Smokehouse Combo $14.00

Stuffed French Toast Combo $15.00

Belgian Waffles $16.00

Double BLT $16.00

Bacon Cheeseburger $17.00

Country Omelette $18.00

Ham & Cheese Omelette $18.50

It has been cooked by poaching it in water.

The waiter or waitress keeps asking if you like the meal in order to get a bigger tip from you.

Would you like anything else?

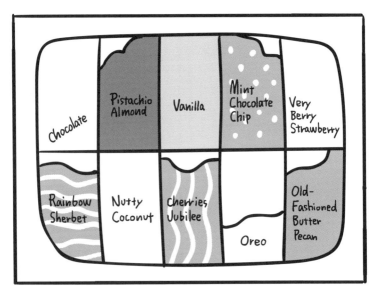

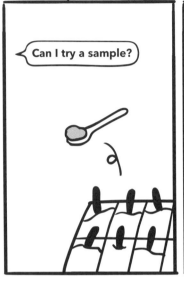

Ordering Ice cream

cone

cup

waffle cup

spoon

scoop

one scoop

Small

Medium

Large

two scoops

Toppings

chocolate

cereal

almond

blueberry

strawberry

sprinkles

29

Excuse me. Does this bus go downtown?

Yes.

Downtown is the central area or commercial center of a town or city.

What time will the bus come?

It will come in 10 minutes.

Bus operators don't carry change, so you'll need the exact fare.

Do you know about TAP cards?

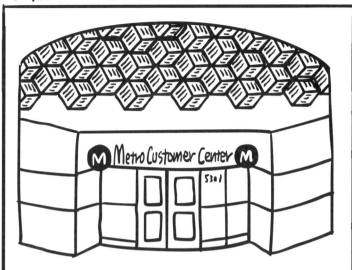

A TAP card is used as a bus or train ticket.
If you need one, go to a Metro Customer Center or any of
the hundreds of Metro Pass sales outlets around town.

I'd like to have
a weekly TAP.

There are 3 types of passes:
day, weekly, and monthly passes.
You simply tap your card each time you board.

There's a bookstore!

I'm looking for *Twilight*.

That should be in the fantasy section.

Do you have this in hardcover?

There are two types of book covers: hardcover and paperback.

Here you are.

It's $10.

Please put it in a bag.

BOOK CATEGORIES

Art

Religion

Children's Books

Teens

Biography

Entertainment

Cookbooks

Architecture & Photography

Home & Garden

History

Business & Money

Self-Improvement

Nonfiction

Fiction & Literature

Graphic Novels

Mystery & Crime

Science & Nature

Science Fiction & Fantasy

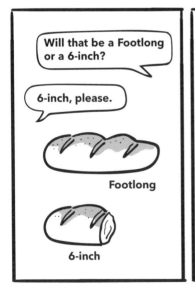

Lay's is one of the most well-known potato chips.

Ordering Sandwiches

**When you order,
you may ask as follows:**

1. Tell the staff the type of bread you want.

white   wheat   Italian   etc.

2. Tell the staff the size of bread you would like.

Footlong (about 30cm)   6-inch (about 15cm)

3. Tell the staff if you'd like it warmed or toasted.

I want it toasted, please.   Warm it up, please.   No thanks.

4. Add cheese if desired.

American   Cheddar   Swiss   etc.

5. Tell the staff what type of vegetables you would like.

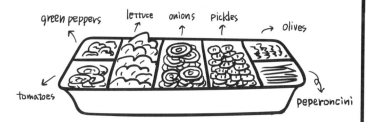

green peppers
lettuce
onions
pickles
→ olives
tomatoes
peperoncini

6. Tell the staff the type of sauce.

barbecue sauce
mayonnaise
mustard
sweet onion sauce

7. Add salt & pepper if desired.

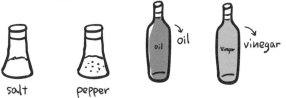

salt
pepper
oil
vinegar

8. Add chips & drinks if desired.

43

A For here, please. → p.13
B Excuse me. Is this seat taken? → p.18
C Come this way. → p.20
D There's something in it. → p.25
E Excuse me. Can I have a to-go box please? → p.25
F Can I get a napkin, please? → p.27
G Excuse me. Dose this bus go downtown? → p.30
H I'm looking for *Twilight*. → p.34
I Please put it in a bag. → p.35
J Put everything on it except onions. → p.39

I'm doin' so well, huh :)

* **On Sale 10% off**
  means you may purchase it 10% cheaper.

* **For Sale**
  means that you are able to buy it.

* **Clearance**
  is a sale to reduce stock, usually for items from the last season.
  You may not get a refund after purchasing them.

48

49

What size are you?

Standard size chart (women)

	XS	S	M	L	XL	XXL
American	0, 2	4, 6	8, 10	12, 14	16, 18	20
Japanese	44	55	66	77	88	*
	85	90	95	100	105	110
Bust	32-33	34-35	36-37	38-40	41-43	*
Waist	24-25	26-27	28-29	31-33	34-36	
Hip	34-35	36-37	38-40	41-43	44-46	

Leg length for bottoms

short

regular

long

extra long

Clothing Categories

parka

tank top

tights

poncho

mini shorts

chiffon skirt

ankle-length skirt

dress

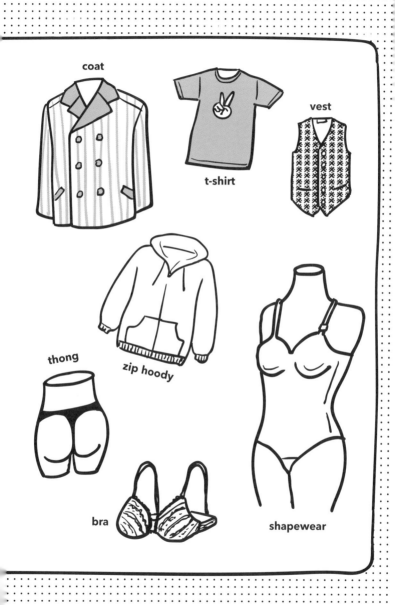

coat

t-shirt

vest

zip hoody

thong

shapewear

bra

When getting a refund

If the item was not what you expected...

When exchanging

I'd like to exchange this for a bigger size.

I'd like to exchange this for a blue one.

I need to exchange this. It has several snags in it.

I'd like to exchange this for a different one.

You need to pay $10 more.

How to use an ATM

1. Insert your ATM card.

2. Select a language.

3. Enter your PIN.

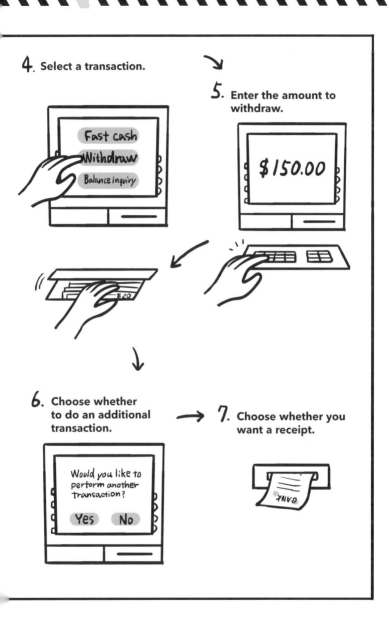

4. Select a transaction.

Fast cash
Withdraw
Balance inquiry

5. Enter the amount to withdraw.

$150.00

6. Choose whether to do an additional transaction.

Would you like to perform another transaction?

Yes   No

7. Choose whether you want a receipt.

BANK

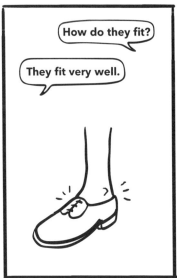

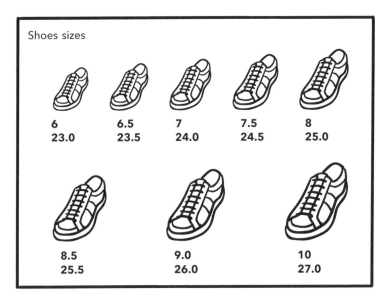

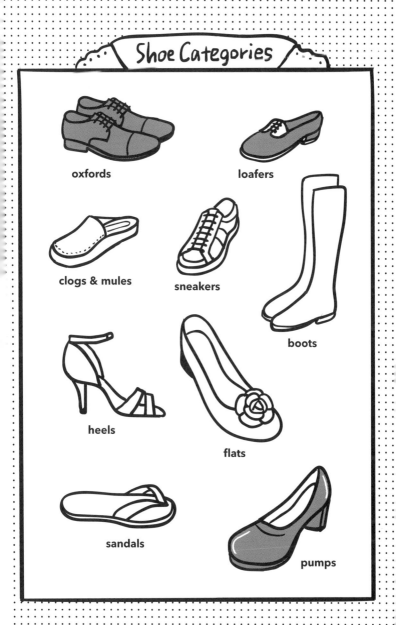

Shoe Categories

oxfords

loafers

clogs & mules

sneakers

boots

heels

flats

sandals

pumps

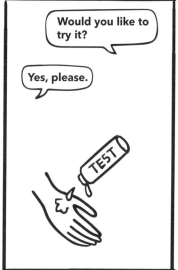

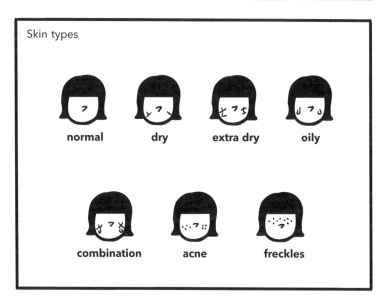

Skin types

normal   dry   extra dry   oily

combination   acne   freckles

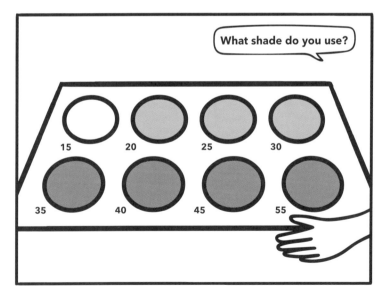

Cosmetic Categories

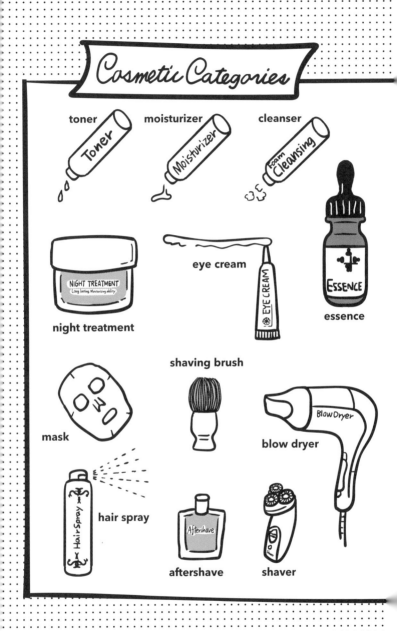

toner

moisturizer

cleanser

night treatment

eye cream

essence

mask

shaving brush

blow dryer

hair spray

aftershave

shaver

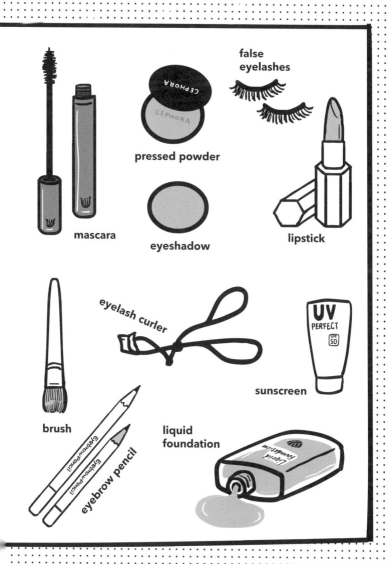

false eyelashes

pressed powder

mascara

eyeshadow

lipstick

eyelash curler

sunscreen

brush

eyebrow pencil

liquid foundation

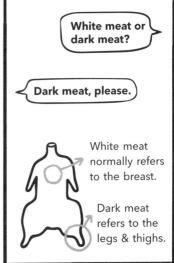

68

Original or crispy?

Crispy, please.

Both original and crispy are deep-fried and crunchy, but crispy is even crunchier.

Drinks?

A medium Coke.

Side dishes?

A biscuit, please.

Here or to go?

Here, please.

coleslaw

potato wedges

mashed potatoes

mac & cheese

biscuits

green beans

corn on the cob

seasoned rice

72

A Do you have this in black? → p.47

B Excuse me. Are you in line? → p.48

C Cash, please. → p.50

D I'd like to exchange this for a different one. → p.55

E Excuse me. Can I try these in a 7? → p.58

F They fit very well. → p.59

G I'll take the brown ones. → p.60

H Can I try this on? → p.65

I Um... combo two, please. → p.68

J Can I have some extra ketchup? → p.70

74

Without a reservation...

Have you booked a table?

No.

How many?

Just one.

There're no seats available at the moment.

Please put your name on the waitlist.

Waitlist

Anna

Are you ready to order?

DINNER MENU

Fried Calamari $10.95
Shrimp Cocktail $13.95
Onion Rings $7.95

Classic Caesar Salad $8.95
Mixed Green Salad $7.95
Chinese Chicken Salad $8.95

Charbroiled Filet Mignon $31.95
New York Strip Steak $29.95
Charbroiled Rib Eye Steak $29.95

Fish and Chips $16.75
Cedar Plank Atlantic Salmon $23.95
Jumbo Lump Crab Cakes $26.95

Penne Pesto $14.95
Angel Hair Pasta Pomodoro $13.95
Broiled Shrimp Pomodoro $18.95

Chicken Quesadilla $13.95
Oven Roasted Half Chicken $16.95
Chicken Piccata $18.95
Grilled Herb Chicken Breasts $16.95

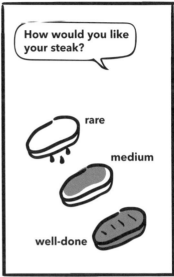

Please bring out whatever is ready first.

MENU

If you want your orders served one by one, you'd better tell your server ahead of time.

How is everything?

Wonderful!

Good.

Not bad...

Are you done? May I take the plates?

I'm still working on it.

Would you like anything for dessert?

No, thanks. I'm full.

Useful expressions

How many?

One.

May I see your ID?

Sure.

JAPAN PASSPORT

Would you like to sit at the bar?

I'd love to.

LIQUOR CATEGORIES

draft beer   dark beer   bottled beer   canned beer

on the rocks   no ice   double   straight-up

red wine   white wine   house wine

lime   lemon   salt   ginger ale   soda

bartender   drunk

What's an OPEN TAB?

At bars in the U.S., you need to pay every time you order with either credit card or cash.

But with an OPEN TAB, you don't have to pay for your drink immediately after ordering.
(a tab = a bill or an account)

1. If you pay by a credit card, you may ask to open a tab.

2. They will hang on to your credit card at the bar.

3. Whenever you order a drink, they'll add it to your bill.

4. When you're ready to leave, pay for your drinks all at once.

Dunn Loring - Merrifield Station

Let's go to Penn Station.

Metro Card

Can you use a Metrocard Vending Machine?

There are two types of MVMs.

Metro Card

← The larger machines accept cash, credit cards, and ATM or debit cards.

The small machines are for credit cards and ATM or debit cards only. They do not accept cash. →

Please be aware that not all stations in NYC make service announcements.
NYC = New York City

Which exit should I take if I'm going to the ABC Museum?

Take exit #(number)3.

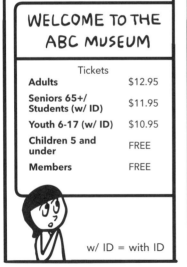

WELCOME TO THE ABC MUSEUM

Tickets	
Adults	$12.95
Seniors 65+/ Students (w/ ID)	$11.95
Youth 6-17 (w/ ID)	$10.95
Children 5 and under	FREE
Members	FREE

w/ ID = with ID

One adult, please.

Asking for a picture of yourself.

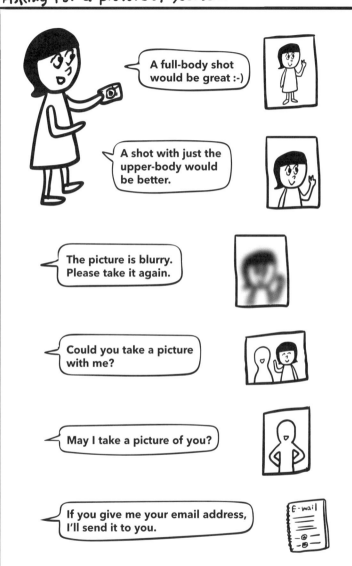

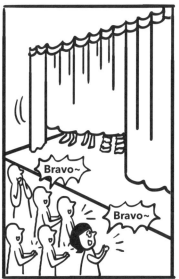

Theater Etiquette

No smoking in the theater.

Videotaping and photography are not allowed during the performance.

No outside food is allowed into the theater.

If you arrive late, you may have to wait for a break during the show before you can be seated.

The audience may go outside during intermission.

THEATER TERMS

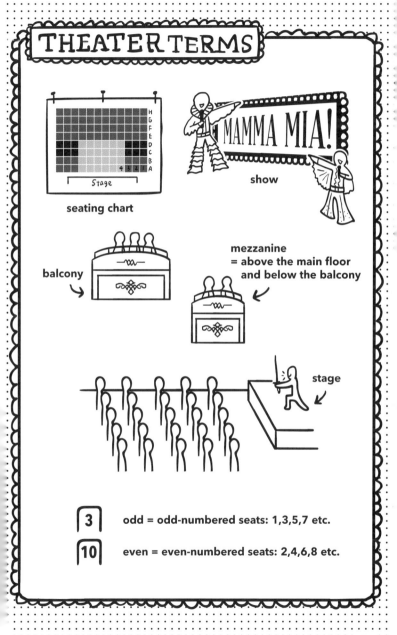

seating chart

show

balcony

mezzanine
= above the main floor
and below the balcony

stage

| 3 | odd = odd-numbered seats: 1,3,5,7 etc. |

| 10 | even = even-numbered seats: 2,4,6,8 etc. |

Hello. I'd like to rent a car.

Okay. What size do you want?

A sedan is like a Corolla.

An SUV is like an X-Trail.

I want an SUV.

A minivan is like a Serena.

The fuel service option is to pay in advance for a full tank of fuel and to bring the car back empty.

E

Yes.

F

Take exit #(number)3.

G

Sure.

H

The appearance of the performers at the end of a performance to receive applause from the audience. Photography is allowed during a curtain call.

A I'd like a non-smoking seat. → p.77
B Yes, at 7:30, under Anna. → p.77
C I'm still working on it. → p.80
D That comes with lime? → p.84
E Is this the right way to Penn Station? → p.88
F Which exit should I take
   if I'm going to the ABC Museum? → p.89
G Excuse me. Could you take a picture of me? → p.96
H It's a curtain call! → p.99
I I prefer the lowest coverage. → p.104
J I'll return it on May 13th. → p.104

110

How to avoid long lines

Some amusement parks offer tickets for popular rides
that can be reserved beforehand.
They allow guests to avoid waiting in long lines.
Below is just one sample procedure of how to issue a
SpeedPass.

1. **Insert your ticket
into the SpeedPass booth.**

2. **A SpeedPass ticket will be
dispensed.**

3. **Your reserved time will be on
the SpeedPass ticket.
If it says, "3:00 to 4:00" then
you may return
at any time within that hour.**

I wanna get something.

This may be pricey. How much is it?

It's $37.

Um...I can't afford it. Sorry. Thanks anyway.

No problem.

Asking for directions.

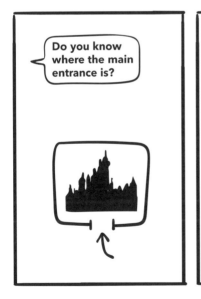

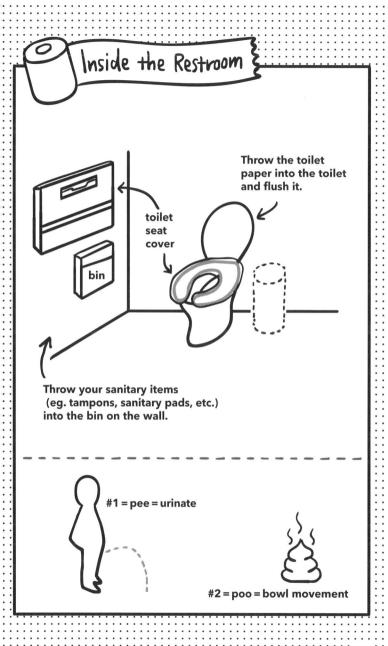

Inside the Restroom

Throw the toilet paper into the toilet and flush it.

toilet seat cover

bin

Throw your sanitary items (eg. tampons, sanitary pads, etc.) into the bin on the wall.

#1 = pee = urinate

#2 = poo = bowl movement

w/o = without

119

Medicine

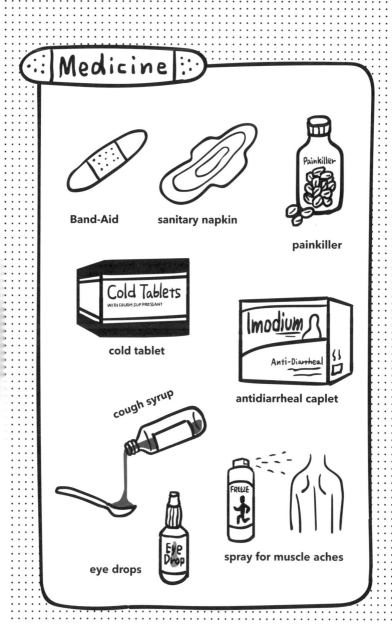

Band-Aid

sanitary napkin

painkiller

cold tablet

antidiarrheal caplet

cough syrup

eye drops

spray for muscle aches

A deposit is a guarantee to cover extra costs such as the mini bar or room damage.

If you don't have a reservation.

Asking about the hotel.

A non-smoking room, please.

What time is breakfast served?

What time is the pool open until?

Do you provide rollaway beds?

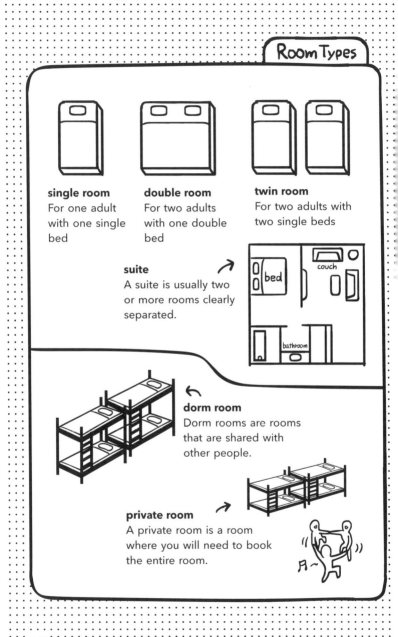

single room
For one adult with one single bed

double room
For two adults with one double bed

twin room
For two adults with two single beds

suite
A suite is usually two or more rooms clearly separated.

bed
couch
bathroom

dorm room
Dorm rooms are rooms that are shared with other people.

private room
A private room is a room where you will need to book the entire room.

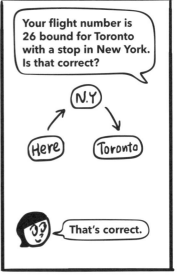

{ Duty Free Items }

fragrances & cosmetics

fashion & accessories

liquor & tobacco

luggage & leather goods

watches & jewelry

electronics

134

On board the plane...

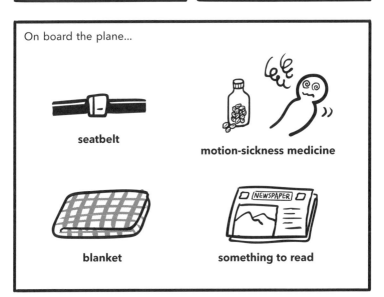

seatbelt

motion-sickness medicine

blanket

something to read

It means to change planes for a connecting flight.

Am I at the right place?

Keep going straight a bit and turn right at the corner.

Attention, all Delto Airlines passengers going to Toronto. We will begin boarding at gate 2 at this time.

140

Keep going straight a bit and turn right at the corner.

A This may be pricey. How much is it? → p.114

B Where is the restroom? → p.115

C Are you in line? → p.116

D I feel somewhat nauseous. → p.119

E Can you take me to the EDISON Hotel? → p.122

F I'd like to check in, please. → p.123

G I'd like a room with a double bed. → p.124

H Would you please help me with this? → p.135

I One more pillow, please? → p.135

J Am I at the right place? → p.138

144

Dictation Book

ディクテーション編

147

Useful phrases when ordering

=   =   =

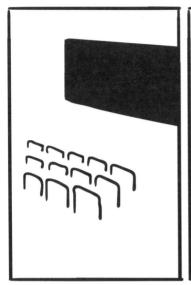

MOVIE CATEGORIES & GENRES

After eating...

Check No. 123457
Tab 234 Guest 1

1.

$

2. $

                    $

        $
        $

+Tip:

=Total:

Would you like anything else?

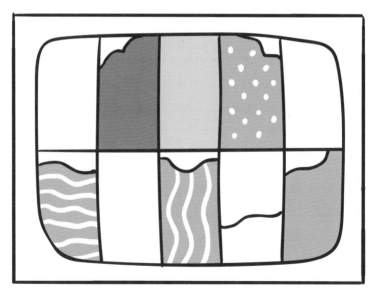

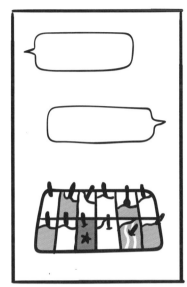

163

164

Do you know about TAP cards?

168

BOOK CATEGORIES

Ordering Sandwiches

1.

2.

3.

4.

5.

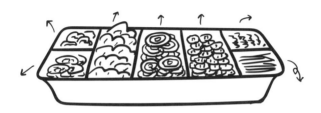

6.

7.

8.

* On Sale 10% off

* For Sale

* Clearance

177

If you pay by credit card...

If you pay by check card...

What size are you?

	XS	S	M	L	XL	XXL
American	0, 2	4, 6	8, 10	12, 14	16, 18	20
Japanese	44	55	66	77	88	*
	85	90	95	100	105	110
Bust	32-33	34-35	36-37	38-40	41-43	*
Waist	24-25	26-27	28-29	31-33	34-36	
Hip	34-35	36-37	38-40	41-43	44-46	

Clothing Categories

When getting a refund

If the item was not what you expected...

When exchanging

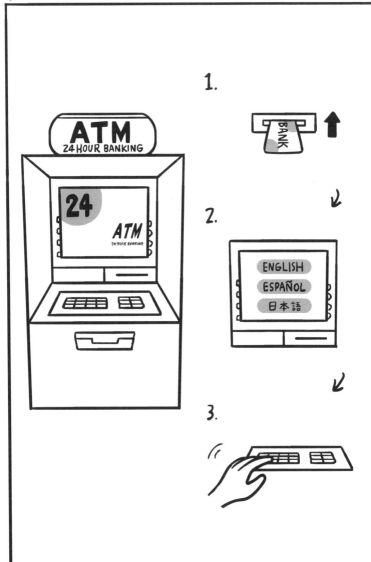

1.

2.

ENGLISH
ESPAÑOL
日本語

3.

4.

5.

Fast cash
Withdraw
Balance inquiry

$150.00

6.

7.

Would you like to perform another transaction?

Yes   No

187

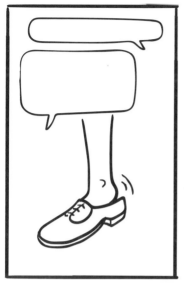

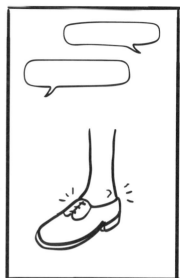

Shoes sizes

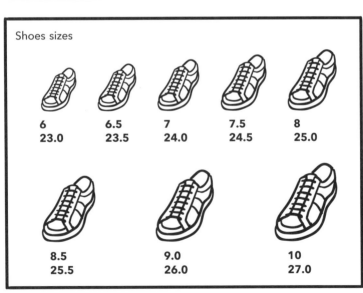

6	**6.5**	**7**	**7.5**	**8**
23.0	**23.5**	**24.0**	**24.5**	**25.0**

8.5	**9.0**	**10**
25.5	**26.0**	**27.0**

Shoe Categories

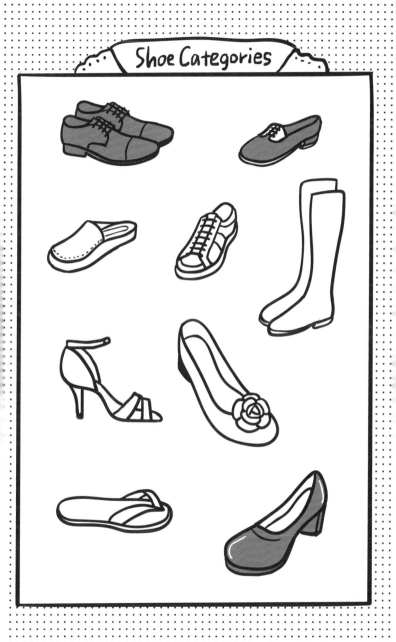

Skin types

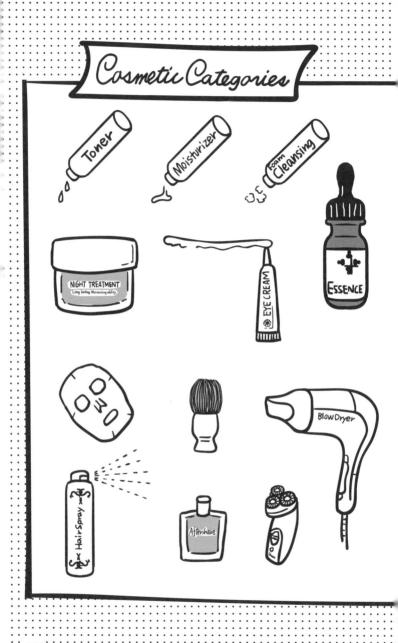

Cosmetic Categories

Toner

Moisturizer

Foam Cleansing

ESSENCE

NIGHT TREATMENT
Long lasting Moisturizing ability

EYE CREAM

Blow Dryer

Hair Spray

Aftershave

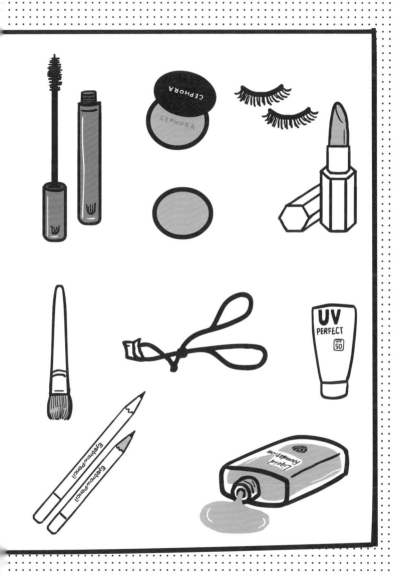

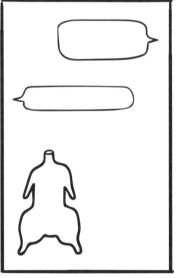

201

Without a reservation...

After a few minutes...

With a reservation...

Useful expressions

208

LIQUOR CATEGORIES

210

What's an OPEN TAB?

1.

2.

3.

4.

Can you use a Metrocard Vending Machine?

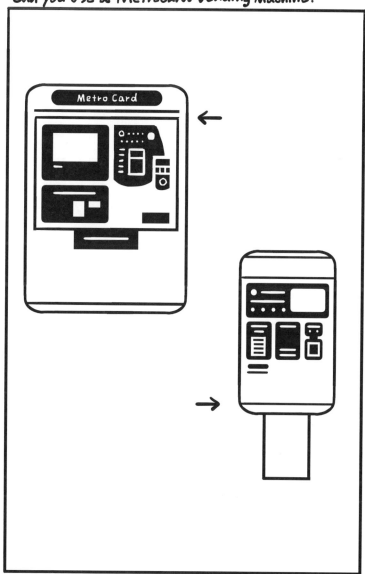

w/ ID = with ID

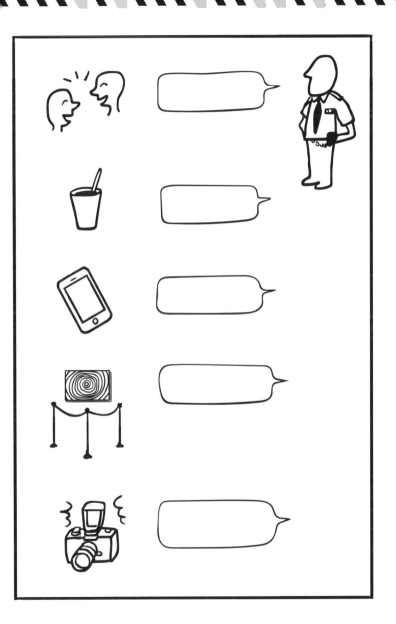

224

THEATER TERMS

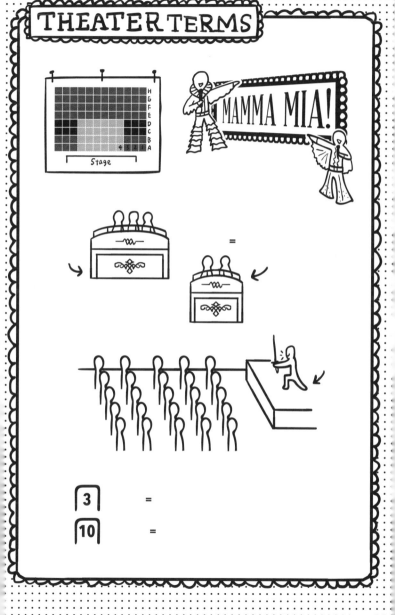

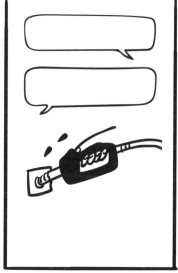

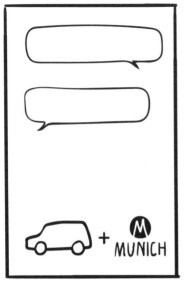

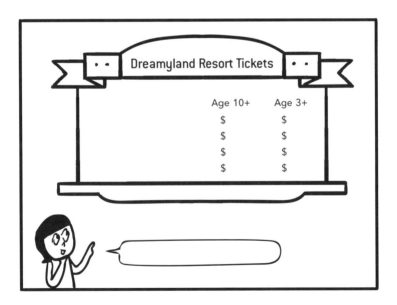

Dreamyland Resort Tickets

Age 10+	Age 3+
$	$
$	$
$	$
$	$

What is the 2-Park ticket?

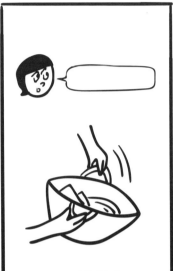

How to avoid long lines

1.

2.

3.

INSERT YOUR
TICKET HERE

RECEIVE
YOUR
TICKET
HERE

INDIANA JOE'S
ADVENTURE

SPEED PASS
Return Anytime Between
3:00 PM
TO
4:00 PM

Asking for directions.

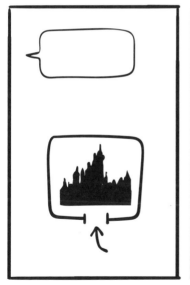

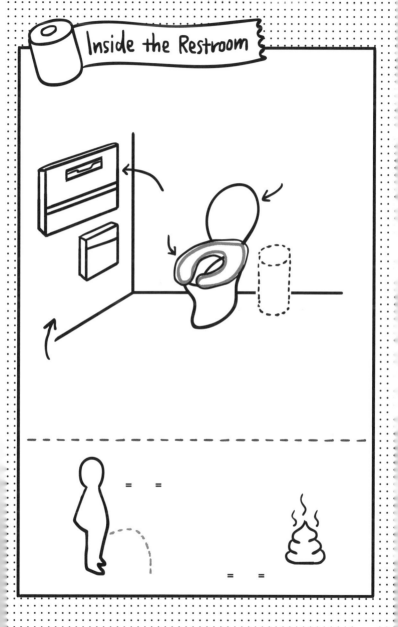

w/o = without

241

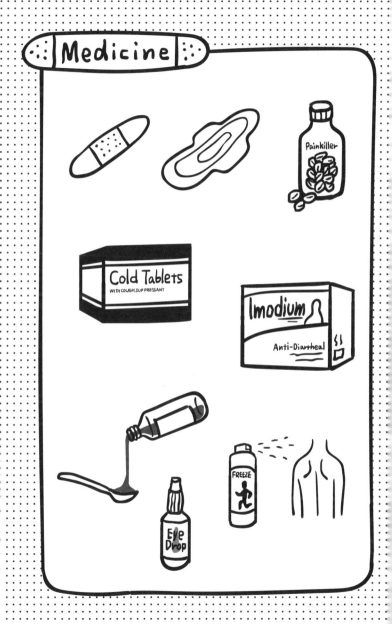

244

If you don't have a reservation.

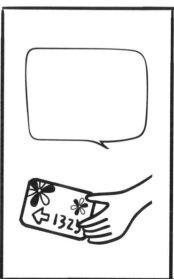

Asking about the hotel.

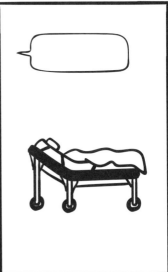

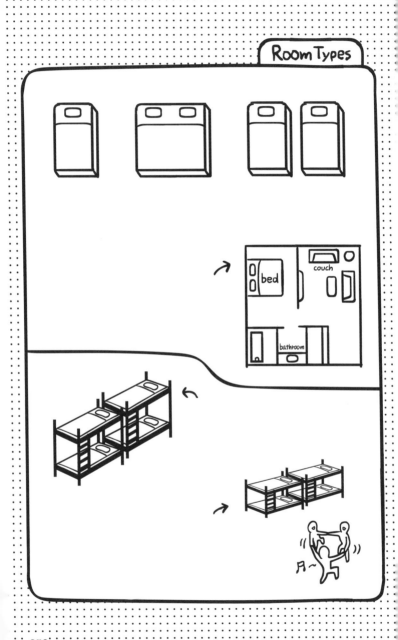

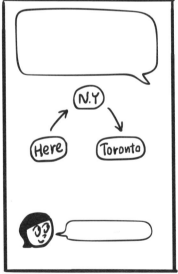

← window

window seat   aisle seat

1st row seat

253

Duty Free Items

On board the plane...

著者

エリー・オー
Ellie Oh

アメリカの現地シニアデザイナー、フィリピンの国際学校
ディレクター、韓国の英語講師および著者として多様な経歴
をもつ。日常のさまざまなシーンに即したリアルな英語と異
文化理解に関心が深い。幼稚園児から社会人、シニアに至る
まで、幅広い年齢層の生徒に教えた経験をもとに「生きた英
語」を伝えるための活動を行っている。

絵でおぼえる英会話　基礎編

2020 年 11 月 17 日　第 1 刷発行

著　　者	エリー・オー
編　　者	ターシャ・キム／アンナ・ヤン
デザイン	小寺練＋小木曽杏子
イラスト	サンダースタジオ
翻訳協力	三嶋圭子
校　　正	株式会社ぷれす
英文校閲	リサ・ウィルカット／原田麗衣
音声録音・編集	ELEC（一般財団法人 英語教育協議会）
編　　集	平沢拓＋一柳沙織
発 行 人	山本周嗣
発 行 所	株式会社文響社
	〒105-0001
	東京都港区虎ノ門 2-2-5　共同通信会館 9F
	ホームページ　https://bunkyosha.com
	お問い合わせ　info@bunkyosha.com
印刷・製本	中央精版印刷株式会社

読者アンケートに
ご回答いただいた方
全員に無料特典を
プレゼント！